SHRIMAD BHAGAVAD GITA

AN ATTEMPT TO SUMMARIZE EACH CHAPTER

DR. JAGADEESH PILLAI

Dedicated to all people seeking wisdom and motivation in despondency.

Contents

Contents

Contents

Prayer

"mayy eva mana adhatsva
mayi buddhim nivesaya
nivasisyasi mayy eva
ata urdhvam na samsayah"

(Bhagwat Gita: Chapter Twelve verse 8)

Sri Krishna declared, "O Arjuna, focus your mind on Me
and direct all your intellect towards Me. In this way, you
will remain in Me without any hesitation."

About The Author

Dr. Jagadeesh Pillai four times Guinness World Record holder, a voracious reader, writer, and true research scholar was born in Varanasi, the abode of Lord Shiva. He is Ph.D. in Vedic Science. He is a multi-faceted polymath with innate qualities, creative ideas and many remarkable achievements. Although his roots extend back to "Gods own Country"(Kerala), the residents of Varanasi feel proud of him and adore him as a child of Varanasi who caters to every individual in need without any expectations. A deep study into his profile reflects that he has added so many feathers to his cap which makes him quite unique. He is a four times Guinness Book of World Records Holder in the following subjects :

1. "Script to Screen" which he achieved by producing and directing a state of art animation film within the shortest time possible by breaking the earlier set record by Canadians. There are many national and international Awards and Recognitions to his credit.

2. Longest Line of Post Cards which he has done on the occasion of 163 years of Indian Postal Day by 16300 post cards. The event was also connected with a questionnaire about Indian Flag.

3. Largest Poster Awareness Campaign – This was achieved by designing an awareness campaign on the subject "Beti Bachao – Beti Padhao".

4. Largest Envelop – Towards tribute to Prime Minister's

initiative 'Make in India' – he has created about 4000 sq meter envelop using waste papers.

5. Attempted by lighting 70000 candles on a 210 kg cake to celebrate the 70th Indian Independence day recorded in World Records India.

6. Attempted a documentary on Dhamek Stupa of Sarnath dubbing in 17 languages, result is waiting from Guinness World Records.

He is versatile in Gita teaching. The young generation is fond of his Gita teaching and he has changed the life of many young through his continued motivational boost up and teachings.

He has composed and sung Gayatri Mantra in 1008 different tunes.

He has composed and sung Hanuman Chalisa in 108 different tunes.

He has composed and sung hundreds of Sanskrit Bhajans, Patriotic songs, etc.

He has written and directed so many short films and documentaries for awareness campaigns.

He has done voluntary services to UP Police and Kerala Police to spread awareness campaigns on the various issue through videos and photography.

He is on the path of authoring thousands of books on Indian culture, Indian Temples, and the life of extraordinary people.

It is hard to believe that he has produced and directed more than 100 Documentaries on a particular city (Varanasi) which is done by a single person.

He has helped and guided more than 25 boys and girls to achieve world records through various creative and innovative methods.

A multifaceted person who can apply the best of his intellect using the God-given blessings which have been showered upon every human being granting them an immense capacity to learn, experience, and experiment with many things and do wonders in this world of discrimination and disparities.

He is a teacher and a student at the same time who always learns every day and teaches every day. As a master, his weakness was that he never sticks to a particular subject. Perhaps this weakness gives him the strength to master any area which he came across.

Each of his days dawned with learning a new topic and he spend most of his time experimenting and researching it.

He is also a selfless social activist and a motivational speaker.

His life was full of struggle, ups and downs, and failures.

But he never gave up and faced all his trials and tribulations full of confidence. Today he is a successful young man with a lot of enthusiasm and rich life experience.

He has sung full Ram Charita Manas 51 hours audio by his own composition. He has also sung the whole Bhagavad-Gita in his own composition with a rhythmic background.

He has also sung "Lokah Samastha Sukhino Bhavantu" in 50 different languages.

Currently working on a detailed and scientific study on Veda, Upanishad, Puranas, Bhagavad Gita, etc.

He has composed and sung Hanuman Chalisa in 108 different compositions and Gayatri Mantra in 1008 different compositions.

Awards

Four Times Guinness World Records

Winner of Mahatma Gandhi Vishwa Shanti Puraskar

Mahatma Gandhi Global Peace Ambassador

Kashi Ratna Award

Dr. APJ Abdul Kalam Motivational Person of the Year 2017

Mother Teresa Award

Indira Gandhi Priyadarshini Award

Bharat Vikas Ratna Award

Udyog Ratna Award

Vigyan Prasar Award

Poorvanchal Ratn Samman

Preface

The Bhagavad Gita is one of the central scriptures from Hinduism and is considered a spiritual guide, helping to show people the path to liberation and inner peace. With such a profound influence and a significant body of wisdom, the Bhagavad Gita has been interpreted and analyzed by many Indian scholars and authors throughout the years, furthering its reach and cultural importance. It contains teachings and moral advice in the form of dialogue between Lord Krishna, an incarnation of the Hindu god Vishnu, and Arjuna, a mortal warrior. Many renowned scholars, authors and thinkers have explored the text in depth and have found inspiration from its messages.

The Bhagavad Gita is a collection of 18 chapters, each exploring traditional Hindu teachings about morality and spiritual wisdom. An attempt to summarize each chapter would be to say that they largely revolve around the protagonist Arjuna's struggles with the idea of fulfilling his duties as a warrior, despite his moral qualms. He is taught by Lord Krishna throughout the book and through this teaching discovers how action and knowledge relate to Dharma (righteousness), which ultimately leads him on a journey of enlightenment. Various concepts such as karma, non-attachment and divine self are also explored in an effort to spark self-reflection in readers. The overall message promised by these lessons is often described as one of liberation — our ability to free ourselves from suffering if we align ourselves more closely with our higher paths and towards liberation from Samsara (the cycle of life).

No doubt, thousands of people have written commentaries on the Bhagavad Gita. In this book, I am also attempting to provide a concise overview of each chapter based on my notes and understanding. I hope to offer a unique perspective on this ancient text, which has been studied and revered for centuries.

This book is an attempt to provide a comprehensive overview of the Bhagavad Gita, one of the most influential and revered texts in Hinduism. Through this book, readers will gain a better understanding of the Gita's teachings and the profound wisdom it contains. Each chapter of the Gita will be summarized in detail, providing readers with a comprehensive overview of the text's main themes and ideas. By the end of this book, readers will have a better appreciation of the Gita's timeless wisdom and its relevance to modern life.

Dr. Jagadeesh Pillai - PhD in Vedic Science - Four Times Guinness World Record Holder

CHAPTER ONE

ARJUNA VISHADA YOGA - The Distress of Arjuna

The Bhagavad Gita is one of the most important sacred texts of India, written in Sanskrit and attributed to the sage Vyasa. It is also called the Song of God. The first chapter of this text is known as Arjuna Vishada Yog, or the Yoga of Arjuna's Despondency. In this chapter we witness a dialogue between Lord Krishna and the Pandava prince Arjuna, taking place on the battlefield at the start of the great war of Kurukshetra.

Arjuna was overcome with despondency on the battlefield, unable to reconcile his duty as a warrior with his own moral code and the idea that he must fight and possibly kill his own family and teachers. Despite Lord Krishna's attempts to persuade him, Arjuna felt heavy in his heart and could not move forward with his mission. Arjuna's experience is a metaphor for the struggles of life and how to reconcile our own needs and feelings with our duties and obligations. In the process, Arjuna comes to understand the true nature of dharma, or righteous action.

Arjuna's despondency was characterized by deep sorrow and despair. He was in a state of panic, not wanting to fight nor wanting to retreat, unable to take any decisive action. He saw the opposing armies filled with his kin, his beloved teachers, and the people of his nation, and the thought of killing any of them caused tremendous anguish. He felt that the war was unjust, seeing no greatness in killing his own family, and his heart sank. He collapsed on his chariot in despair, exclaiming that all his goals and ambitions had become insubstantial.

The Bhagavad Gita's first chapter serves as a guide for making the correct decision, providing an explanation of dharma and how it applies in Arjuna's scenario. Lord Krishna reveals to Arjuna his divine identity and persuasion with the ultimate truth. He explains that Arjuna's questions and dilemmas, though challenging, have already been resolved and that he has no need to be despondent. Krishna advises Arjuna to accept his duties, free his thoughts of concerns of future results, and fight only to uphold the values of dharma.

Thus, the Bhagavad Gita chapter 1 is a powerful exploration of facing one's duty while not succumbing to despair. In Arjuna's struggles we can see a reflection of our own journey in life and the lessons we must learn to overcome our doubts and fears. Despite his despondency, Arjuna was capable of finding hope and inner strength through Krishna's words, and eventually emerge from his despair to carry out what was rightfully expected of him.

DR. JAGADEESH PILLAI

"The Bhagavad Gita is not just a book; it is the essence of religious thought, the essence of the ancient culture of India." - Madhav Bhatt

Madhav Bhatt's quote emphasizes the importance of the Bhagavad Gita in Hindu culture. This quote emphasizes the depth of wisdom and understanding to be gained from the teachings of the Bhagavad Gita. It encourages readers to seek out its profound teachings and incorporate them into their lives, as it can provide a great source of spiritual knowledge.

CHAPTER TWO

SANKHYA YOGA - The Yoga of Knowledge

The second chapter of the Bhagavad Gita, called Sankhyayoga, brings together themes of knowledge and action, or jnana and karma. This chapter marks the introduction of yoga, as well as an exposition on the nature of the physical, mental and spiritual realms. This discussion centers on the three pathways (dharmas) of renunciation (sannyasa), devotion (bhakti), and action (karma).

The text begins with Arjuna asking Krishna about the soul and spirit, to which Krishna responds with a declaration on the divine unity of all creation. He speaks of a single force that permeates all things and originates from beyond the bounds of time and space. This force sustains the whole physical universe and is the source of both material and spiritual life. From this force comes three paths (dharmas) of renunciation (sannyasa), devotion (bhakti) and action (karma). All of these paths lead to moksha, or liberation from the cycle of rebirth.

Krishna then explains the different dharmas and their characteristics. He defines the path of renunciation (sannyasa) as that of unwavering spiritual detachment and devotion (bhakti) as serving the divine with total surrender. The path of action (karma) involves following the prescribed rituals and duties laid out in the Vedas. This path is particularly important to Arjuna's current situation, as he is a warrior whose path is to fight in the great Mahabharata war.

Krishna acknowledges the importance of each path, but warns Arjuna against imbalanced spiritual practice as it can lead to attachment and hinder him from finding liberation. To illustrate, he explains the three different kinds of desires — sattva, rajas and tamas — which correspond to light (sattva), activity (rajas), and darkness (tamas). Krishna advises Arjuna to balance his yoga practice of these three paths.

Krishna then offers his guidance on the path of yoga, which entails practicing the eight steps of ashtanga yoga. These steps involve breath control (pranayama), meditation, concentration (dharana), and various physical postures and poses (asanas). This practice enables us to gain a calm, settled mind and brings about self-realization, or Atman.

The chapter concludes with Arjuna's vow of embracing the path of yoga and dedicating himself to its practice. As such, the chapter offers readers a guide to practice yoga and remain on the path of wisdom, knowledge and action. This path brings about liberation from the material and spiritual shackles, ultimately bringing about moksha or salvation.

DR. JAGADEESH PILLAI

"The Bhagavad Gita is the most precious gift from ancient India to modern man; its light of eternal truth will guide humanity for generations to come." - S Radhakrishnan

S Radhakrishnan's quote is a testament to the lasting impact that the Bhagavad Gita has had on India and the world. This quote serves to show how the wisdom of the Bhagavad Gita has been passed down through generations and how it will continue to influence people's lives. It is a reminder that one can continue to seek out these profound teachings and reflect on them throughout their life.

CHAPTER THREE

KARMA YOGA – The Yoga of Action

The third chapter of Bhagavad Gita, 'Karma Yoga', looks at the concept of Dharma and how it helps us to achieve liberation from the cycle of suffering. Karma Yoga, or union with the divine through enlightened action, is integral to the Bhagavad Gita's message. In this chapter, Lord Krishna communicates the importance of action in accordance with Dharma—one's natural rights and obligations as a human being. He explains that an individual should strive to act virtuously while at the same time remaining unattached to the outcome of those actions.

Karma Yoga involves the cultivation of a devotional attitude towards Dharma and carries the notion that all action is an offering to the Divine. This, according to Lord Krishna, is the key to understanding the concept of liberation. Lord Krishna explains, in this chapter of Bhagavad Gita, that an individual should do their duty without expectation of reward, offering every action to God with reverence and trust. The notion of 'striving without attachment' carries a spiritual component, as it is only when one can transcend attachment to the fruits of their actions that true realization can be attained.

Moreover, cultivating a sense of selflessness is essential to understanding Karma Yoga. True happiness, explains the Bhagavad Gita, cannot come from external sources, but must come from within. In other words, it is only through the act of surrendering to the Divine and executing one's actions with a sense of selfless devotion that one can come to understand true liberation. In this chapter, Lord Krishna also stresses the need to perform one's duty with integrity and respect in order to preserve one's dignity. He further warns against yielding to temptation and selfish desires, as these can lead to suffering.

Ultimately, the third chapter of Bhagavad Gita communicates an enlightening message of how Dharma and Karma Yoga are connected. Through faith and virtuous action, one can strive towards true inner peace. By understanding the importance of Karma Yoga and the virtue of selflessness, an individual can attain the ultimate enlightenment of liberation.

"The teachings of the Bhagavad Gita are a reminder that we are surrounded by eternal truths, and that those truths should not be forgotten." - Purnima Madhavan

Purnima Madhavan's quote emphasizes the timelessness and universality of the teachings found in the Bhagavad Gita. This quote highlights the importance of utilizing these teachings to gain a better understanding of ourselves and our purpose in life. It serves as a reminder that these profound teachings are accessible to all and can be used by anyone looking for guidance.

CHAPTER FOUR

GYANA KARMA SANYASAYOGA- The Yoga of Renunciation of Action through Knowledge

The Bhagavad Gita is one of the most important Hindu scriptures, written in Sanskrit and consisting of 18 chapters. The fourth chapter consists of Jñāna–Karma-Sanyasa yoga, which is a complex set of teachings on achieving spiritual liberation. It focuses on understanding our true nature and the transient nature of all worldly things, as well as on developing renunciation and enlightenment. It is also a practical guide to developing moral and spiritual virtue in our everyday lives.

At the start of the chapter, Arjuna is overwhelmed with the thought of having to fight his relatives and expresses his doubts about the true path to liberation, so Krishna advises him to take the path of Jñāna–Karma-Sanyasa yoga. Through this, Arjuna can come to find peace by understanding the true nature of suffering. Throughout the chapter, Krishna explains the need for one to renounce physical desires and be focused on spiritual goals to reach the highest levels of liberation.

Krishna firstly explains that although performing rituals and meditating is necessary, this alone can not lead to liberation. One must also strive to understand the true essence of humans and their relationship with the Divine through meditation. This means learning to know the true self, realising the importance of self-care and contemplation, and living in the present moment rather than clinging to the past or future.

Krishna goes on to describe the importance of forbearance and devotion. By remaining pure in thought and word, one can make the most out of their spiritual experience. This leads to a profound understanding of the purpose of one's actions and how to focus on their goals from a place of wisdom and humility. Through renunciation, one can create situations that do not lead to attachment but instead lead to liberation.

Finally, Krishna speaks of detachment. Detachment can be seen in the way one approaches their utterances, thoughts and feelings. Detachment is key in avoiding being attached to the outcome of any action and focusing instead on what has been consciously decided to be beneficial.

The four chapters of the Bhagavad Gita offer a detailed and practical guide to liberation. Through the teachings of Jñāna–Karma-Sanyasa yoga, Krishna stresses the importance of understanding our true self and developing renunciation and enlightenment. This is necessary in order to make the most out of our spiritual experience and ultimately, strive for spiritual liberation.

"The Bhagavad Gita is the sacred book of Hinduism, and it stands as a symbol of the highest wisdom and understanding." - Saurabh Dixit

Saurabh Dixit's quote is a testament to the value of the Bhagavad Gita in Hinduism. This quote serves to emphasize the importance of the teachings of the Bhagavad Gita in Hindu culture and how it is seen as a powerful source of wisdom for benightment.

CHAPTER FIVE

KARMA SANYASA YOGA - The Yoga of Renunciation

Karma-Sanyasa Yoga is the fifth chapter of the Bhagavad Gita, where Lord Krishna counsels Arjuna on the path of action, which is central to the pursuit of long-term success and completion of goal-reaching tasks. Through both instruction and example, the Lord elucidates the fundamentals of Karma-Sanyasa Yoga, the act of performing one's duties without expecting or seeking pleasure or reward in return, and approaching life with an attitude of sannyasa, or inner liberation.

At the beginning of this chapter, Arjuna is paralyzed by the thought of having to fight against his own family, and thus wishes to shirk his duties. Lord Krishna encourages him to perform his dharma, or duty, and to "stand and fight", lest he call himself a coward. This underlying message can be applied to our modern world, emphasizing the importance of facing our obligations and responsibilities in spite of our personal inclination or convenience.

Lord Krishna further emphasizes the need to overcome the dualities and illusions of day-to-day life, extolling Arjuna to rise above material interests and attachments and realize his true identity as Atma. This realization of the Atma, or inner soul, is the starting point of an individual's journey towards achieving freedom from life's many distractions. This freedom is a result of achieving total detachment from all material possessions and achieving a spiritual oneness with the universe.

The key message of Karma-Sanyasa Yoga revolves around inner freedom and peace. According to Lord Krishna, exercising self-control and overcoming emotion are critical components of inner liberation. Arjuna must remain equanimous even in the midst of great distress, abstaining from himself and materials alike. He advises that Arjuna must not become attached to either joys or fears, success or failure, as none of these bring real happiness or achieve the ultimate goal.

Ultimately, the point of Karma-Sanyasa Yoga is to fully realise our true identity, our purpose in life, and to reject all material attachments. It is to arise above the dualities and illusions of this cruel world and to attain inner liberation by practicing detachment and self-control. Practicing this philosophy will provide individuals with the inner freedom they need to pursue true happiness, while simultaneously accomplishing their duties without any obligations or expectations.

"The Bhagavad Gita is the essence of the Vedas and Upanishads". -Mahatma Gandhi

Mahatma Gandhi, who led India's struggle for independence, considered the Bhagavad Gita to be the essence of Hinduism. He was of the opinion that all the other scriptures, even though important, were secondary to the teachings of the Bhagavad Gita. He found solace, strength, and inner peace by reading the Gita and often quoted it in his speeches and writings.

CHAPTER SIX

DHYANAYOGA – The Yoga of Meditation

Gita 6th Chapter, commonly referred to as 'Dhyana Yoga', is an important text within Hinduism. It provides teachings on the nature of meditation and its practice as a spiritual discipline. According to the Gita, through the practice of meditation, one can consciously connect to the deeper spiritual reality of our existence, connecting one to the inner-Source of their own existence, and to the inner essence of the universe. The chapter focuses on four core areas of meditation, including contemplation, experiential insight, unified emotion and tapasya, or self-control.

In the sixth chapter, Lord Krishna first explains the value of contemplation. This is seen as being paramount to the success of a person in their spiritual practice. He sets out the importance of contemplation over action, and presents the need for further study and contemplation to come to the realisation of how to develop the true self. He further explains the focus needed to bring about the realisation of one's essential Truth. In addition to contemplation, the Gita sets forth the use of experiential insight as another foundation of successful meditation.

In the sixth chapter of the Gita, Lord Krishna further sets out the importance of deep and sustained control over one's emotions as a tool towards connecting with one's true self. He talks of a single-minded focus which helps to move away from the values of the world, and towards the Unified Self. Further, he explains the need for tapasya, which involves controlling the mind and desires. By controlling our desires and mastering our mind, we can detach from emotions and move closer to our essence. In addition to the practice of tapasya, Lord Krishna also speaks of the importance of self-reflection in order to remain mindful of the underlying purpose of meditation.

Finally, the Gita speaks of the need for an unified approach to meditation and encourages practitioners to focus on the path as a whole. He explains that the inner journey should be undertaken with an attitude of devotion, piety and awareness in order to maintain focus and commitment to the practice. In summary, Gita 6th Chapter is a profound and insightful piece of writing, providing invaluable guidance on a meditative path of spiritual awakening and enlightenment. Through four key areas of contemplation, experiential insight, unified emotion and tapasya, it provides a foundation to help practitioners to access their true personal power and to open their mind and heart to the greater Truth of existence.

"That man attains peace who, having abandoned all desires and attachments, moves through the world free from hopes and fears". -Swami Vivekananda

Swami Vivekananda, one of the most influential spiritual leaders of India, made it his mission to spread the knowledge of the Gita to the world. This quote sums up one of the most important teachings in the Bhagavad Gita: renouncing material objects and developing no attachment to them is essential to attain inner peace and harmony.

CHAPTER SEVEN

GYANA VIGYANAYOGA - The Yoga of Knowledge and Judgment

The seventh chapter of the Bhagavad Gita, entitled "Jnana–Vijnana Yoga," is a dialogue between Arjuna, a great warrior and Krishna, a supreme divine being. This chapter focuses on the concept of wisdom that comes from self-realization. Through this dialogue, Arjuna is taught to remain unperturbed in the face of both happiness and sorrow, and to detach himself emotionally and morally from materialism and the ego.

Krishna begins the chapter by emphasizing that only the wise can determine how their destiny is to be played out; those with a lack of understanding will be overpowered by their emotions, and overwhelmed by the course of their lives. He then explains the power of "the true nature of the Self," which is beyond materialism and the mind. It is only by understanding this true nature of the Self that one can be liberated from the bonds of materialism and ego.

Krishna further explains that unknowledgeable people get lost in their own emotions, which drive them towards personal gains known as "the external pleasures." Hence, Arjuna is advised to be free from those emotive desires and make a distinction between real and unreal situations. He further teaches Arjuna to overcome the fear of death by realizing that one's body is merely a temporary vessel, and that death is an inevitable part of the cycle of life.

Krishna further explains the importance of meditation and wisdom in understanding the true nature of existence. He emphasizes that one should remain engrossed in knowledge, so that one can understand the real purpose of life, and that one should take refuge in the higher Self, instead of the body or mind.

He concludes this chapter by explaining the power of the Yogis – those who reach the path of liberation through knowledge and unwavering devotion.

In summary, the seventh chapter of the Bhagavad Gita stresses the importance of wisdom gained through self-realization. Through this dialogue, Arjuna is advised to be liberated from the bonds of materialism, be free of emotive desires, understand the real purpose of life, and remain engrossed in knowledge and unwavering devotion. The wisdom of this dialogue breaks free the shackles of a mundane life and leads one to the path of liberation.

"One should not be moved by joy and grief, by heat and cold, by honour and dishonour; battling the enemies of attachment, fear and anger, one should remain established in the Self". -Adi Shankara

Adi Shankara was an influential Hindu Teacher who translated and interpreted many of Hindu scriptures. This quote on Bhagavad Gita reflects his belief that in order to be spiritually evolved, one has to learn to take joy and grief alike and to be independent from external influences.

CHAPTER EIGHT

AKSHARA BRAHMAYOGA - The Yoga of the Imperishable Brahman

The eighth chapter of Bhagavad Gita, titled Aksara-Brahma Yoga, explains the importance of realizing one's true self in light of the knowledge of the imperishable Brahman. The entire chapter is focused on the topic of Brahman and its role in self-realization.

The chapter starts with Krishna describing the indestructible Brahman as the cause of all existence. He then further explains that all the differences between souls, such as the distinctions of caste, race, and gender, are mere appearances. He reveals that all souls are part of an eternal, changeless whole which is Brahman. In order to realize this ultimate truth, an individual needs to steady their mental and physical functions, as well as their faculties of knowledge and action. He also instructs Arjuna to practice Brahmanism, where one learns to free themselves from the cycle of birth and death, and thereby achieve freedom from suffering.

Krishna then illustrates the concept of Brahmanism by comparing it to rain, which is both invisible and indestructible. Rain is the same regardless of its form, whether it is liquid or manifested in the form of dust and then remerges as a liquid, it is still the same entity. He uses this analogy to explain that just as one identifies the rain, one should similarly be able to identify one's self with imperishable Brahman.

Krishna further explains that a person who is devoted to Brahman will eventually find ultimate freedom. Such a person will experience transcendental joy and be able to perceive the true nature of the universe without bias or attachment.

Krishna emphasizes the importance of realizing one's true self in light of knowing the imperishable Brahman. This will help one to lead a life of purpose, striving to overcome their attachment to the material world and instead finding the joy of eternal existence. He further assures Arjuna that his teachings will free him from misery, shaping him into a liberated being. He further explains that Brahmanism is not to be dreaded, rather embraced, in order to attain the ultimate truth and peace.

Through this chapter, Krishna has given us an important spiritual lesson, which is to practice Brahmanism to free ourselves from the cycle of death and rebirth, and also experience ultimate peace. He has also encouraged us to strive for self-realization and to discover our true selves with the knowledge of the imperishable Brahman.

"The secret of the Bhagavad Gita is the knowledge of five basic truths which form the science of the soul". -A. C. Bhaktivedanta Swami

A.C. Bhaktivedanta Swami was a prominent religious figure who worked tirelessly towards spreading the messages of the Gita across the world. This quote shows his belief that the essence of the Gita is the understanding of five basic principles: activity, renunciation, knowledge, wisdom, and devotion.

CHAPTER NINE

RAJA VIDYA RAJA GUHYAYOGA -The Yoga of Sovereign Science and Sovereign Secret

The Bhagavad Gita, the sacred Sanskrit text belonging to the Hindu tradition, is the cradle from which Indian philosophical ideas originally arose. Widely considered to be one of the most important spiritual texts in Hinduism, the Gita comprises eighteen chapters divided among three sections known as 'Guna', 'Karma' and 'Gyana'. The ninth chapter, Raja Vidya Raja Guhyaya, is a part of the second section and explains the nature of the Supreme Reality and its relation to the individual person, as expounded by Lord Krishna.

In this chapter, Lord Krishna begins by explaining that worshipping of Him is the surest way to attain eternal knowledge, which will lead one to Supreme Reality. He explains that the Supreme Reality is a state of complete perfection, bliss and knowledge, and one should aim to imitate this state in one's own life. He also explains that the spirit of knowledge is the highest of all beings and is like a great ocean of ever-flowing divine light and power, beyond the comprehension of all perception and imagination. This divine knowledge can only be obtained by those whose hearts are pure and devoted to Lord Krishna.

Lord Krishna states that he is the source of both knowledge and ignorance. He explains that when one understands He is the source of both and accepts the knowledge He imparts, the darkness of ignorance is destroyed and the pure light of knowledge is revealed. Directing the attention towards desire-free actions and pure intent, the yogi succeeds in gaining perfect mastery over his senses and eventually attains the greatest knowledge.

Lord Krishna further explains that he is the creator of both virtuous and evil actions and encourages the followers to remain indifferent and rise above all desires, anger, fear and every form of duality and change. He stresses that one should remain in a meditative state and free from all dualities. He also explains that there is no difference between wisdom and ignorance, since both are only mere expressions of the same Supreme Reality.

In short, the ninth chapter of the Gita conveys the teachings of Lord Krishna about the power of knowledge and how it leads one to the attainment of true wisdom and divine knowledge. It teaches that one must remain determined and devoted to the practice of yoga in order to reach the highest state of knowledge and be able to gain complete mastery over one's senses. By practicing this Raja Vidya Raja Guhyayoga, one can be liberated from the cycle of birth and death and eventually be united with the all-pervading Supreme Reality.

"The Bhagavad Gita is the most systematic statement of spiritual evolution of endowing value to mankind. It is one of the most clear and comprehensive summaries of perennial philosophy ever revealed; hence its enduring value is subject not only to India but to all of humanity." – Alduous Huxley

CHAPTER TEN

VIBHUTI YOGA – The Yoga of Divine Manifestations

The Gita, one of the most revered holy scriptures of Hinduism, is a beautiful and timeless treatise expounding on a range of spiritual, philosphical and personal growth topics. Chaper 10 of the Gita, the Vibhutiyoga Yoga of Divine Manifestations, is an incredibly profound and thought-provoking chapter, which takes the reader on a deeper journey in their spiritual discipline. This chapter speaks of the divine, how to identify and partake in it, and the importance of its role in our lives.

This chapter begins by presenting Arjuna's curiosity and his yearning to understand the divine. He recounts the wonders of the divine, inquiring if there is anything more powerful or grand that can be found. Krishna lovingly offers a reply and begins his discourse on divine manifestations.

Krishna begins this discourse by breaking down the

concept of the divine into three primary aspects. The first aspect is that of the Vishvarupa, or the All-Pervading Omnipresent form of the divine. This pertains to the divinity which pervades all of Nature, the essence that binds all creatures and elements together. The next aspect is of the embodied self, the body incarnation that each being is infused with to represent their spiritual essence. The final aspect is of the universal Self, the ultimate Creator and Sustainer of reality. Krishna also mentions that the divine manifests through a variety of forms and levels, which is what gives it its timeless and expansive nature.

These three aspects form the foundation of Krishna's explanation, which is then further explored through a discussion of the fundamental qualities of the divine. One example comes from the recognition of devotion, the loyalty and fidelity to God that results in blessings and spiritual growth. Krishna gives the example of himself, mentioning how he sacrificed himself many times to protect the world, a trait that serves as a model of devotion that allows us to foster our own relationship with the divine.

Krishna emphasizes the importance of understanding the divine, and how it is imperative for us to develop our relationship with it. He explains that upon understanding the divine, one is able to transcend the boundaries of the physical body and witness the grandeur of a one Oneness with everything. In this state, one is free from afflictions such as anger and envy, and instead bask in a serene, unparalleled bliss.

In conclusion, chapter 10 of the Gita is an incredibly rich

and annotated exploration of the divine, one which reveals the poetic beauty, mystery and power that lies beneath the esoteric depths of the reality of our oneness. This chapter teaches us to pursue and of course, nourish our relationship to the divine, as it is through understanding the divine that we can hope to gain an appreciation for its unlimited potential, and be blessed with a life of inner peace and growth.

"When doubts haunt me, when disappointments stare me in the face, and I see not one ray of hope on the horizon, I turn to Bhagavad-Gita and find a verse to comfort me; and I immediately begin to smile in the midst of overwhelming sorrow." – Mahatma Gandhi

CHAPTER ELEVEN

VISHVARUPA DARSHANAYOGA - The Yoga of the Vision of the Cosmic Form

The 11th chapter of The Bhagavad Gita, known as Vishvarupa Darshan Mahatmya, is a crucial part of the spiritual mission of Lord Krishna. In this chapter, Krishna reveals his divine form to Arjuna. This event marks the climax of Arjuna's spiritual journey and It is the tipping point in Arjuna's transformation.

The Vishvarupa Darshan Mahatmya is an important part of The Bhagavad Gita because it displays the all-encompassing wisdom of Krishna as the ultimate Supreme Being. The chapter begins when Arjuna, overwhelmed by his battle with his family, requests that Krishna show him his divine form. Krishna then creates a hazy darkness that swallows Arjuna and transports him to the divine court, where he sees his true form for the first time.

Krishna reveals himself as the source of all creation and represents the limitless power of Brahman. Arjuna, feeling overwhelmed by the sight of Krishna's divine form, faints in awe of his majesty and beauty. Krishna then explains to Arjuna the meaning behind his cosmic form, teaching him the nature and scope of the divine, from which all of existence emanates and into which it dissolves. By demonstrating his divine form, Krishna reveals that all beings, however grand or small, originate and return to him; the great ocean of existence.

The visvarupa darshan also reveals to Arjuna the true nature of the cycle of life and death. Krishna stresses the importance of spiritual knowledge, above material gain and desires. He also explains how to attain liberation from the cycle of birth and death, by performing selfless deeds without attachment to the ego and without fear.

This chapter of The Bhagavad Gita is truly essential to understanding the divine power and cosmic cycle of existence. The vision of Vishvarupa is an awe-inspiring sight that brings about the transformation of Arjun and gives him a greater insight into the power of Brahman. By witnessing this grand display of Brahman's power, Arjun not only gains an appreciation for Brahma's vastness, but also a deeper understanding of one's own existence in the divine realm. It is a profound experience that enables Arjuna to see beyond the boundaries of the material world and understand the oneness of all creation.

"You have a right to perform your prescribed duty, but you are not entitled to the fruits of action. Never consider yourself the cause of results of your activities, and never be attached to not doing your duty." – Albert Einstein

CHAPTER TWELVE

BHAKTI YOGA - The Yoga of Devotion

Bhakti yoga, or the way of love and devotion, described in the Twelfth Chapter of the Bhagavad-Gita is considered one of the greatest philosophies of spiritual practice and transformation. Bhakti Yoga is based on the highest form of devotion to a chosen God or Divine entity and is the path of unconditional love and surrender. The path of Bhakti consists of chanting devotional hymns, meditating on one's chosen Deity, and saying prayers of gratitude and offering one's actions in service to God.

Bhakti Yoga begins by first recognizing the divine presence within oneself, then expressing that love and devotion through humble and selfless acts of service or sacrifice. It is through this path that one can let go of all material desires in exchange for spiritual surrender. In Bhakti Yoga, the beloved is God, and the devotee is the Self. When both co-exist, nothing can exist between them. This is the essence of Bhakti – Unity with God.

The path of Bhakti involves forsaking attachment to temporary things in life and surrendering the ego to the

Lord. Instead of living in the purposeless pursuit of pleasure and material gain, one offers their life in service to God; following his will instead of their own desires. This spiritual surrender leads to a life filled with peace and contentment, regardless of the life situations.

Bhakti Yoga is a direct path to enlightenment, where spiritual realizations happen in an easier and more powerful way. Through Bhakti Yoga, one's attention is constantly directed towards God, so that the divine Presence is felt in all of the activities of life. One's consciousness becomes one with God, thereby eliminating the distinction between the two. As one becomes focused on devotion to God, the spiritual practices eventually become second nature and the soul experiences a sense of freedom and joy.

Bhakti Yoga is sometimes called the easiest path to liberation because it involves the simple practices of chanting and singing the Lord's names, offering prayers and meditating deeply. Regardless of whether one is a beginner or an advanced practitioner, Bhakti Yoga is a powerful practice for spiritual transformation. Thus, practicing Bhakti Yoga leads to a blissful and sacred relationship between one's inner self and the Divine.

"Bhagavad Gita has a profound influence on the spirit of mankind by its devotion to the truth and its revelations."
– Herman Hesse

KSHETRA KSHETRAGYA VIBHAGAYOGA - The Yoga of Difference between the Field and Field-Knower

The thirteenth chapter of the Bhagavad Gita begins with Arjuna asking Lord Krishna to explain the divisions of Kshetra and Kshetragya. Krishna then provides detailed descriptions of the two concepts and explains the differences between them.

First, Krishna states that Kshetra is the field of activities, which consists of all three worlds: the physical, the mental, and the spiritual. This field is made of the five elements (earth, water, fire, air and ether), the soul, and the faculties of perception, action and knowing. He further explains that all of these elements are controlled by the influence of the three attributes: Sattva, Rajas, and Tamas.

Krishna then goes into detail about Kshetragya, or "the knower of the field". He explains that this is the person aware of the field, or the person who understands the purpose and importance of the five elements, the soul and the faculties. This is the supreme conscious being, and he has perfect knowledge of everything.

In order to illustrate these two interrelated concepts, Krishna gives an analogy. He explains that the body is the field and the soul is its knower, whereas the senses are the charioteer that guides us in our work.

He then goes on to explain what happens when a person gains knowledge of the field and the knower: they become liberated and attain a level of eternal bliss. This is the highest state, attained by those who understand both the field and the knower, and there is no further to go.

Ultimately, the thirteenth chapter of the Bhagavad Gita provides excellent insight into the concepts of Kshetra and Kshetragya. It explains in detail the difference between the field and the knower and clarifies how they work together to lead an individual to true liberation and bliss. It provides a beautiful illustration of the interconnectedness between these two principles, and offers a way for an individual to reach the highest level of consciousness. As such, it is a valuable passage to reflect upon and ponder upon.

"Happiness is a state of inner fulfillment, not the
gratification of inexhaustible desires for outward things."
– Ralph Waldo Emerson

GUNATRAYA VIBHAGAYOGA – The Yoga of the Division of Three Gunas

Although Bhagavad Gita is one of the most important sacred texts in Hinduism and is universally known for its vast philosophical wisdom, it is most famous for its introduction to the idea of dharma and the three 'gunas'. Chapter fourteen of the Bhagavad Gita, also known as 'Gunatraya Vibhaga Vibhaga' or the 'Division of the Three Gunas' is most renowned for its teachings, examining the philosophical basis of dharma.

The three gunas or qualities explained in this chapter are the three fundamental proclivities of mind and are referred to as the three stages of human behavior in their cosmic forms ojas, sattva, and tamas. Ojas is described as the highest and most desirable quality, possessing qualities such as contentment, truth, and religious detachment. Sattva is the second gunas with similar qualities but is less complete and more exclusive, in contrast to ojas. Lastly, tamas is the lowest state, where one is overwhelmed with negative emotions such as anger and hatred.

The dialogue between Lord Krishna and Arjun explores the notion of dharma and the three gunas which are the underlying principle of action in human life. The chapter describes these qualities in detail, from the type of food to be eaten to the type of action to be performed. It explains the importance of activities such as listening to the Scriptures, being devoted to one's Guru or spiritual teacher, performing japa or meditating, controlling the mind, and controlling the senses.

Lord Krishna emphasizes the importance of sattva guna, placing it at the apex of the status of three gunas. He explains that to achieve total success a man must always strive to maintain sattvic behavior, keeping a balance between ojas and tamas. He further explains the disadvantages of tamasic behavior, warning that it should not be encouraged.

'Gunatraya Vibhaga' therefore provides an in-depth look into the three fundamental qualities of the human mind and reveals the importance of dharma in guiding one's moral conscience. Chapter fourteen demonstrates that for an individual to act in purusartha, or in pursuit of religious merits, he must adopt qualities of sattva guna. Lord Krishna emphasizes that this is the only means to gain ultimate peace, true joy, contentment, and harmony in one's life.

In conclusion, the 'Division of the Three Gunas' explains the complex structure of human behavior in order to obtain true spiritual knowledge and understanding of existence. Each individual needs to recognize the three gunas in their spiritual journey and strive to harmonize them in order to live in independence, freedom and happiness.

"From a clear knowledge of the Bhagavad-Gita all the goals of human existence become fulfilled. Bhagavad-Gita is the manifest quintessence of all the teachings of the Vedic scriptures." – Swami Vivekananda

CHAPTER FIFTEEN

PURUSHOTTAMAYOGA - The Yoga of the Supreme Purusha

Gita 15th chapter Purushottamayoga, or "the yoga of the Supreme Purusha", is a central concept in Hindu philosophy that explains the relationship between God and humanity. It is explained in the fifteenth chapter of the Bhagavad Gita, an ancient Hindu text. The chapter focuses on Krishna's dialogue with Arjuna, in which he is instructed to assume a particular yogic posture in order to realize his divine nature as the Supreme Purusha.

The purpose of the yoga of the Supreme Purusha as described in the Gita is to foster a deep inner union between the Self or Atman and the Godhead, or Brahman. This is done through an inner devotion that seeks to align one's consciousness with the divine or ultimate reality. In this way, it is a form of spiritual practice that seeks to demonstrate that all souls are intrinsically connected to the divine consciousness of Brahman. The ultimate goal of this union is to liberate the individual from the cycle of death and rebirth and to bring them to a state of perfect bliss and divine understanding.

Krishna explains in the Gita that the yoga of the Supreme Purusha is not something that can be achieved through mere physical practice or meditation. Rather, it requires a state of inner devotion and perfect surrender in order to open oneself up to the divine energy within. To begin this process, one must first understand the concept of Dharma, or one's life purpose, and work to align oneself with this divine path. This is done by eliminating all selfish desires, attachments, and attachments to the material world, and instead focusing on the true essence of one's inner self.

Upon achieving this state, the Supreme Purusha is revealed to the individual and the true nature of their relationship with the divine is revealed. Through this union, the individual is able to experience perfect bliss and a state of enlightenment in which they gain a deep understanding of the true meaning of their life. In this way, the yoga of the Supreme Purusha can ultimately lead to spiritual realization and liberation from the cycle of death and rebirth.

In conclusion, the fifteenth chapter of the Gita, Purushottamayoga, or the yoga of the Supreme Purusha, is a deeply spiritual concept integral to Hindu philosophy that outlines the relationship between the individual and the divine. Through the practice of yoga, one can find inner peace, spiritual connection, and liberation from the cycle of death and rebirth.

"The Bhagavad-Gita is the most beautiful, perhaps the only true philosophical song extant in any known tongue...Perhaps we can never achieve a perfect contentment and peace until we have learned the lessons taught by Arjuna to Krishna." – Henry David Thoreau

DAIVASURA SAMPAD VIBHAGAYOGA - The Yoga of the Division between the Divine and the Demonic

The sixteenth chapter of the Bhagavad Gita is focused on the distinction between the divine and demonic natures. Krishna explains to Arjuna that a person's nature, whether it be divine or demonic, is dependent on their activities, mental state, and past life's experiences. The path they choose can be either of those two qualities. Krishna reveals that certain qualities are associated with the divine nature and others with the demonic nature.

Divine qualities are those associated with virtue, self-control, courage, austerity, cleanliness, fidelity, and simplicity. They illustrate a life that is focused on the moments and not driven by desire. This path of action is beneficial for those seeking peace, freedom from the bonds of karma, and the ultimate reward of spiritual liberation (moksha).

Conversely, those who choose the path of the demonic nature are described in the Bhagavad Gita as greed, anger, and pride. This path is often motivated by impure desires, such as money, power, and status. It is a response to life that is based on expectations and ego rather than understanding, compassion, and love.

Krishna explains that if a person lives a life whose actions are divinely based, then they can expect to experience joy, freedom of the soul, development of spiritual intelligence, and even freedom from the cycle of karma and rebirth. On the other hand, if they embrace the nature of selfishness and desire, they will experience suffering, bondage, and rebirth in lower orders of life.

The message of the Gita is clear: Choose the path of the divine nature in order to reap its associated rewards. Those who choose the path of the demonic will only find misery, unhappiness, and bondage to their desires. By learning to recognize one's own divine nature, or the inner voice of the soul, one is better able to understand the purpose of their life and the laws of karma. This understanding leads to liberation from the cycle of life and death.

"The Bhagavad-Gita has a profound influence on the spirit of mankind by its devotion to the truth and its revelations." – Hermann Hesse

CHAPTER SEVENTEEN

SHRADDHATRAYA VIBHAGAYOGA - The Yoga of the Threefold Faith

The Bhagavad Gita, one of the most influential texts in Hinduism, is highly valued for its major focus on morality and right action—which is exemplified in the seventeenth chapter, "Shraddha Traya Vibhaga Yoga," or the "Yoga of the Three-Fold Practice of Faith." Within this chapter, Krishna teaches Arjuna the importance of a threefold faith—a faith in one's self, one's actions, and in the highest source of power, God. He gives an in-depth look at the essential components of the threefold faith and its importance in one's path to righteousness.

Krishna states that the three components of a threefold faith are associated with either of the three bodies. The first of these components is faith in the body (or physical). He explains that this body is transient, temporary, and subject to the cycle of life and death. Therefore, one must not become attached to this body, and instead tap into the power of the eternal soul, or mind.

The second component is faith in the mind (or intellectual). This faith involves understanding that symbols and symbols of power within the universe, such as the sun and moon, are manifestations of God's power and will. Furthermore, one must understand that power of the self is attained through good deeds and thoughtful behaviour.

The last and third component, faith in the soul (or spiritual), is an understanding that there is a spiritual power within each of us, shaped by the divine. By tapping into this source, one is able to transform negative energy into positive energy, and it is this energy which will help one along the path of righteousness.

Through a threefold faith, one can learn to exist in balance and harmony. This practice includes prioritizing one's relationship with God and understanding that a person is composed of three distinct parts which must be cultivated in order to achieve true spirituality. Krishna explains that it is the combination of the physical, intellectual and spiritual realms which is necessary for one to gain full access to the higher power within and walk the path of righteousness.

The idea of a threefold faith is highly significant to Hinduism and can be seen as a sort of guide for everyday life. Krishna's teachings encourage practitioners to explore their physical, mental and spiritual selves in order to reach a greater understanding of life. While the Bhagavad Gita does not explicitly say which faith is superior or most beneficial, it does demonstrate that a combined approach is ideal for personal and spiritual development.

"The Bhagavad Gita is the essence of all the scriptures and is a complete guide to practical life. It is a book of universal truths that transcends all boundaries of nations, religions and cultures." – Paul Brunton

CHAPTER EIGHTEEN

MOKSHA SANYASAYOGA – The Yoga of Liberation and Renunciation

The eighteenth chapter of the Bhagavad Gita is titled Sanyasa-yoga, or Liberation by Renunciation. In this chapter, Lord Krishna begins to speak about the ultimate goal of life and the ways of achieving it. The Sanyasa-yoga or the path of liberation through renunciation is discussed in the eighteenth chapter. It is the distillation of the principle of yoga which is to lead a life of balanced activity. According to Lord Krishna in the Gita, the soul can be released from the cycle of existence and death by actively engaging in the services of God and separating itself from the material bonds that keep one attached to the life of cycle of existence and death.

The first verse of the chapter explains the importance of giving up the desire for possessions, reputation, and personal fame, and then following the spiritual path towards Lord Krishna. The true aim of life should be to win the favour of Lord Krishna and seek the assurance of his protection. According to Krishna, this is the only way to attain emancipation and liberation from the cycle of life and death. The path of renunciation starts with the idea of living without too many attachments to material comforts and engaging oneself in the service of God with full faith and devotion.

The second chapter of the Bhagavad Gita focuses on the need to become completely detached from the material world. It explains that the only way to achieve emancipation is to become detached from the objects of attachment. A person practising the path of sanyasa yoga should develop dispassion towards money, material possessions, and relationships. Such a person should give up the material desires and rid himself of the affects of the senses and develop a sense of spiritual detachment. This kind of detachment is necessary to make spiritual progress.

The third chapter discusses the idea of samadhi, which is the ultimate goal in Hinduism. It is the state of absolute concentration and detachment from the material world. This state of being is the ultimate liberation from material bondage and can only be achieved through sanyasa yoga.

The fourth chapter discusses the importance of directing one's desires and attachments towards Lord Krishna and becoming like him by serving him with full devotion. Lord Krishna says that the one who lives in the spiritual world without being attached to material objects finds ultimate liberation. Such an individual can then live peacefully in the Lord's presence and can attain moksha or salvation.

In conclusion, the eighteenth chapter of the Bhagavad Gita explains the importance of following the path of sanyasa yoga or liberation through renunciation to gain freedom from the bonds of materialism and find peace in the Lord's presence. It is the path of righteous action, devotion and detachment from the material world, which can lead to eternal freedom and happiness.

"You have the right to perform your prescribed duties, but you are not entitled to expect results." – Bhagavad Gita 2:47.

This quote has much to do with the idea of Dharma, or duty. It is by performing one's prescribed duties in life that one can truly lead a meaningful and fulfilled life, not necessarily by pursuing a specific set of ends. This quote speaks to the idea of effort and hard work without attachment to the outcome, in that one should focus on the journey rather than the destination.

Other Books Of The Author

1. The Moments When I Met God
2. Kashiyile Theertha Pathangal
3. GURU GYAN VANI
4. Abhiprerak Gita
5. ASSI SE JAIN GHAT TAK
6. Hopelessness of Arjuna
7. The Soul and It's True Nature
8. Sense of Action (Karma)
9. Action through Wisdom
10. Action through Wisdom
11. THEORY AND PRACTICAL OF EVERY ACTION
12. LOGICAL UNDERSTANDING OF THE SUPREME
13. THE IMPERISHABLE SUPREME
14. Yatra Nishadraj se Hanuman Ghat Tak
15. Yatra Karnatak Ghat se Raja Ghat Tak
16. Yatra Pandey Ghat se Prayagraj Ghat Tak
17. Yatra Ranjendra Prasad Ghat se Dattatreya Ghat Tak
18. YaatraSindhiya Ghat se Gwaliar Ghat Tak
19. Yatra Mangala Gauri Ghat se Hanuman Gadhi Ghat Tak
20. Yatra Gaay Ghat Se Nishad Ghat Tak
21. MAA GANGA, GHATEN EVM UTSAV
22. Ganga Arti Dev Deepavali evam Any Utsav
23. Potentials of Digitalized India
24. VEDIC CONSCIOUSNESS
25. A Brief Introduction to Vedic Science
26. Kashi ke Barah Jyotirling
27. IMPACT OF MOTIVATION
28. Let's have a Milky Way Journey
29. Color Therapy in a Nutshell

30. Rigveda in a Nutshell
31. Yajurveda in a Nutshell
32. Samveda in a Nutshell
33. Atharva Veda in a Nutshell
34. Ayushman Bhava - Ayurveda
35. Srimad Bhagavad Gita and Upanishad Connection
36. Shrimad Bhgavad Gita

Contact

DR. JAGADEESH PILLAI

PhD in Vedic Science

Four Times Guinness World Record Holder

Winner of Mahatma Gandhi Vishwa Shanti Puraskar and
Global Peace Ambassador

9839093003

myrichindia@gmail.com

drjagadeeshpillai@facebook

drjagadeeshpillai@instagram

jagadeeshpillai@youtube

www. JAGADEESHPILLAI.com